Tiny-Spiny Animals ABC

Lola M. Schaefer

Heinemann Library
Chicago, Illinois

© 2004 Heinemann Library
a division of Reed Elsevier, Inc
Chicago, Illinois

Customer Service 888-454-2279
Visit our website at www.heinemannlibrary.com

Designed by Sue Emerson, Heinemann Library; Page layout by Que-Net Media
Printed and bound in the United States by Lake Book Manufacturing, Inc.
Photo research by Scott Braut

08 07 06 05 04
10 9 8 7 6 5 4 3 2 1

Library of Congress Cataloging-in-Publication Data
Schaefer, Lola M., 1950-
  Tiny-spiny animals ABC / Lola M. Schaefer.
    p. cm. – (Tiny-spiny animals)
  Summary: Presents an alphabet of things related to spiny animals from A for ant, food for echidnas, to Z for zooplankton, which contains sea urchin eggs.
   ISBN 1-4034-3246-5 (HC), ISBN 1-4034-3509-X (Pbk.)
  1. Animals–Juvenile literature. 2. English language–Alphabet–Juvenile literature. 3. Sea urchins--Juvenile literature. 4. Porcupines–Juvenile literature. 5. Horned toads–Juvenile literature. 6. Tachyglossidae–Juvenile literature. [1. Armored animals. 2. Alphabet.] I. Title.
  QL49.S255 2003
  428.1–dc21

2003002076

Acknowledgments
The author and publishers are grateful to the following for permission to reproduce copyright material:
p. 3 Hans & Jusdy Beste/Animals Animals; p. 4 Donna Ikenberry/Animals Animals; p. 5 Joe McDonald/Animals Animals; p. 6 Jan C. Taylor/Bruce Coleman Inc.; p. 7 Jurgen & Christine Sohns/FLPA; p. 8 E. R. Degginger/Animals Animals; p. 9 Taxi/Getty Images; p. 10 Randy Morse/Animals Animals; pp. 11, 17 DP Wilson/FLPA; p. 12 Michael Bisceglie/Animals Animals; p. 13 Biophoto Associates/Photo Researchers, Inc.; p. 14 D. Robert Franz/Bruce Coleman Inc.; p. 15l Andrew J. Martinez; p. 15r A. B. Joyce/Photo Researchers, Inc.; p. 16 Jen and Des Bartlett/Bruce Coleman Inc; p. 18 Courtesy of High Resolution X-Ray CT Facility, University of Texas at Austin; p. 19 R. Van Nostrand/Photo Researchers, Inc.; p. 20 Scott Johnson/NHPA; p. 21 Laura Riley/Bruce Coleman Inc.; p. 22 H. Taylor OSF/Animals Animals; p. 23 (row 1, L-R) Donna Ikenberry/Animals Animals, Corbis, Jeff Rotman/Photo Researchers, Inc., Fred McConnaughey/Photo Researchers, Inc.; (row 2, L-R) Joe McDonald/Animals Animals, David Welling/Animals Animals, P. Parks/OSF/Animals Animals, Courtesy of Skulls Unlimited; (row 3, L-R) Corbis, Heinemann Library, D. Robert Franz/Bruce Coleman Inc., H. Taylor OSF/Animals Animals; (row 4, L-R) Scott Johnson/NHPA, Taxi/Getty Images, Heinemann Library; back cover (L-R) D. Robert Franz/Bruce Coleman Inc., P. Parks/OSF/Animals Animals

Cover photographs by (L-R) Michael Bisceglie/Animals Animals, Randy Morse/Animals Animals, David Welling/Animals Animals

Every effort has been made to contact copyright holders of any material reproduced in this book. Any omissions will be rectified in subsequent printings if notice is given to the publisher.

Special thanks to our advisory panel for their help in the preparation of this book:

Alice Bethke,
Library Consultant
Palo Alto, CA

Eileen Day, Preschool Teacher
Chicago, IL

Kathleen Gilbert,
Second Grade Teacher
Round Rock, TX

Sandra Gilbert,
Library Media Specialist
Fiest Elementary School
Houston, TX

Jan Gobeille, Kindergarten Teacher
Garfield Elementary
Oakland, CA

Angela Leeper,
Educational Consultant
Wake Forest, NC

Some words are shown in bold, **like this.**
You can find them in the picture glossary on page 23.

A a Ant

Some echidnas eat ants.

They dig for ants with their **claws.**

B b Barb

Porcupine **quills** have **barbs** on the ends.

Barbs are sharp and pointed.

C c   Claw

claws

Porcupine feet have five **claws.**

Porcupines use their claws to climb trees.

D d Desert
E e Echidna

Deserts are hot, dry places.

Some echidnas live in the desert.

F f   Forest
G g   Gnaw

Porcupines find food in **forests.**

They gnaw on tree bark
and branches.

H h   Horn

horn

Horned toads are a type of lizard.

They have **horns** on their heads.

I i Invertebrate
J j Jellyfish

Jellyfish are **invertebrates.**

Jellyfish float in the ocean above the sea urchins.

Kk   Kelp

Sea urchins eat **kelp.**

Kelp is a plant that grows in the ocean.

Ll Larvae

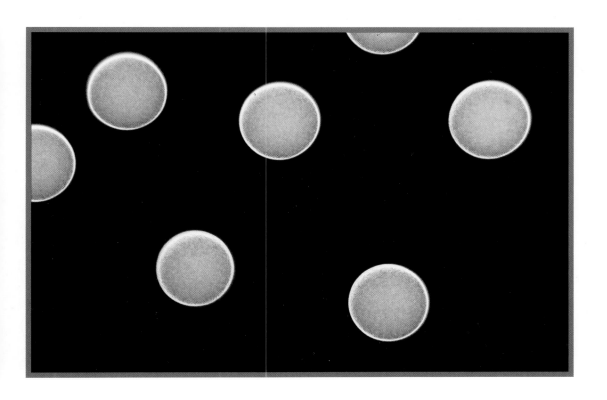

Female sea urchins lay eggs.

Baby sea urchins called **larvae** come out of these eggs.

M m Mouth
N n Nut

teeth

Porcupines' mouths have sharp teeth.

Their teeth help them eat hard foods, like nuts.

O o   Ocean

Sea urchins live in the ocean.

They use their **spines** to stay safe.

P p   Porcupette
Q q   Quills

quills

Baby porcupines are called **porcupettes.**

When they are born, their **quills** are soft.

R r   Round

sea urchin

echidna

Sea urchin shells are round like a ball.

Echidnas can roll into the shape of a ball.

S s   Sticky
T t   Tongue

tongue

Echidnas use their sticky tongues to catch food.

Echidnas eat ants and other bugs.

U u Underside

teeth

The mouth of a sea urchin is on the underside of its body.

There are five teeth in a sea urchin's mouth.

V v Vertebrate

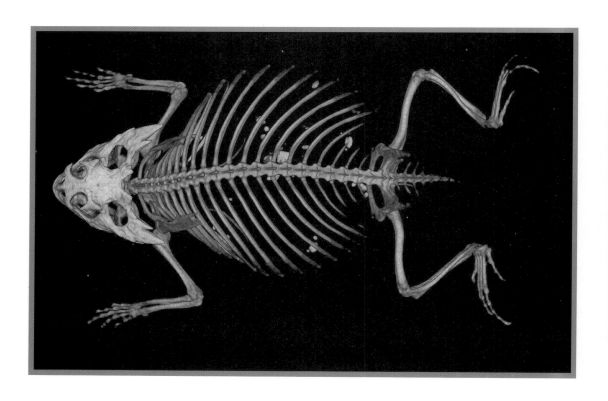

Horned toads are **vertebrates**.

Vertebrates have bones in their bodies.

W w   Worm

Horned toads dig in loose dirt.

They catch worms with their sticky tongues.

Xx   Exoskeleton

exoskeleton

A hard shell covers the sea urchin's body.

This shell can also be called an **exoskeleton.**

Yy Young Echidna

A young echidna hatches from an egg.

A young echidna can fit in your hand.

Z z Zooplankton

Zooplankton is all the tiny animals floating in the ocean.

Sea urchin **larvae** are part of zooplankton.

Picture Glossary

barb
page 4

forest
page 7

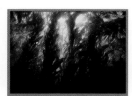

kelp
page 10

spine
page 13

claw
pages 3, 5

horn
page 8

larvae
pages 11, 22

vertebrate
(VUR-tuh-brate)
page 18

desert
page 6

invertebrate
(in-VUR-tuh-brate)
page 9

porcupette
page 14

zooplankton
page 22

exoskeleton
(EX-oh-SKELL-uh-tuhn)
page 20

jellyfish
page 9

quill
pages 4, 14

23

Note to Parents and Teachers

Using this book, children can practice alphabetic skills while learning interesting facts about tiny-spiny animals. Together, read *Tiny-Spiny Animals ABC.* Say the names of the letters aloud, then say the target word, exaggerating the beginning of the word. For example, "/r/: Rrrr-ound." Can the child think of any other words that begin with the /r/ sound? (Although the letter x is not at the beginning of the word "exoskeleton," the /ks/ sound of the letter x is still prominent.) Try to sing the "ABC song," substituting the *Tiny-Spiny* alphabet words for the letters a, b, c, and so on.

! CAUTION: Remind children that it is not a good idea to handle wild animals. Children should wash their hands with soap and water after they touch any animal.

Index